Shawley Nott:
Comic Tales
from
England's Strangest Village

First Edition

Copyright © 2013 Jeff Wiseman

Jeff Wiseman has asserted his right to be identified as the author of this Work in accordance with the Copyright, Designs and Patents Act 1988.

ISBN: 978-1-291-55893-7

CONTENTS

Introduction

I have been asked to isolate my favourite event during my twelve-month stay in the strange English village of Shawley Nott. Was it meeting the fortune-teller who read the future in crushed biscuits? Was it the discovery of the Brotherhood of the Headless Chicken and the antics of Grand Master Feathered Rear? Was it the zombies, cream tea wars, poltergeists or the Helicopter Training School for Rabbits?

The decision is, of course, impossible. My stay in Shawley Nott was the most bizarre of my life and the finer bite-sized incidents are presented here for your consumption. Peculiar, paranormal, eccentric and comedic – words which describe both the events and the villagers. From embroidery circles to crop circles, and the Bermuda Triangle to the Shawley Nott Parallelogram, I hope you find it unbelievably funny.

Jeff Wiseman

1

1. January

Fear, Fillings and the Future – a chat with a Fortune Teller

"I've seen a terrifying things in a chocolate digestive," warns Madame Shortbread, the Shawley Nott Fortune Teller, who no longer uses standard methods after staggering into her tent one night, tripping over her box of tea leaves, rolling across the table on her crystal ball and getting thrown inside her chest of astral predictions. Ever since then she has used her talents to read the future in crushed biscuits. Her clients place their favourites on the table, and she smashes them to pieces with her mallet.

"For holiday advice, bring some oatcakes," she insists. "I crushed one client's oatcakes and told him he'd be taking a trip across the sea, to an eerie landscape, where spectacular cliff faces would pass before his eyes. He went to the USA and fell in the Grand Canyon. How accurate was that!"

Apparently, no two biscuits crush the same. "You have to look at breakage, fusion, crumb angle and proliferation. Fillings, raisins, chips and icing can all be influential. I daren't tell you the scariest story," she says, although relents after a brief discussion and a small payment. "Well, I crushed a fruit and nut crumble, and the result was a face – two raisins for eyes and a peanut for a nose. The client suddenly screamed because it was the spitting image of her late Aunt Cecilia. I told her not to exaggerate, but she showed me a photo, and the odd thing is that her Aunt actually had two raisins for eyes and a peanut nose due to an unfortunate accident in a food-packing factory. The chances of that!"

Madame Shortbread's tent is a small red and white striped affair, standing next to the Post Office. "I get asked lots of things," she continues, "Who am I going to marry? Is my future bright and rosy? Should I send this recorded delivery?"

Has she any advice for those who lack her special insight? "Yes. Don't bring me any biscuits filled with marshmallow. It absorbs impact and on the recoil I've knocked myself unconscious with my own mallet. Twice."

Ghosts and Things that Go Pop

Shawley Nott's local aristocrat is Lord Harbinger of Doom. The Doom Estate is to the north of the village, and his mansion became haunted after a character-building 'Murder Weekend' was held there two years ago for twenty employees of a sales company. The objective was 'to find the strengths, weaknesses and psychological profiles of fellow workers', but unfortunately an accounts manager proved to have the psychological profile of a serial killer, and there were only two survivors. Also, several members of Shawley Nott's Women's Institute disappeared in the mansion only last week whilst admiring the building's interior features, and their ghostly voices can still be heard, with comments like "Mind how you go Doris", "Don't worry, we'll find our way out eventually", and "I'm sure pushing that panel has taken us behind the wall".

Lord Harbinger himself is quite reclusive and never really recovered after losing his left eye to a champagne cork. His younger brother, Harry, taunted him for years with the words 'Give me the bottle before you have someone's eye out', until sadly throwing himself from the mansion roof after Lord Harbinger had suggested they undertake a rare night-time tile inspection together. We should also not forget the tragic death of his father, who tried valiantly to introduce non-native mammals to British soil and was eaten by a puma whilst trimming the Estate roses. Lord Harbinger's art collection holds one very famous family portrait, painted in 1885, showing a bearded, horned and evil-looking central figure, identified by historians as his great-great-grandmother.

Off record, there are known to be several skeletons in the Doom family cupboard, not least because Lord Harbinger's ancestors were very unwilling to cough up for funeral expenses. One negotiation is illustrated in a series of letters to the village undertaker, with each piece of Victorian correspondence requesting a further reduction in burial costs as 'since my previous letter there is now less remaining of my late cousin'.

Dr Grogg and Figgy, his Psychic Hamster

Dr Theodore Grogg, the village physician, specializes in identifying unusual conditions. He has diagnosed patients in Shawley Nott with Gibson's Clang, Lobohalitosis (a complaint that makes human breath smell like that of a werewolf), and Osteoxylophonics, an even rarer condition that allows a patient's ribcage to be struck with sticks to produce a delicate harmony. Grogg also believes in visual diagnostics, with "You look fine. Come back next week if you don't feel any better" being his favourite comment.

In order to see him you first have to speak to his receptionist, who repeats your request ("You'd like to see the doctor?") as though you've just volunteered to cut off your ears with a hacksaw. Dr Grogg occasionally warms his stethoscope by placing it under Don Juan, his tom cat, although if the cat then refuses to budge a whole appointment can be spent listening to the cat purring. One patient pointed out that the doctor ought to be listening to his chest, but Grogg replied "Probably, but the cat sounds healthier, more relaxing, and is considerably more attractive."

He did one famous house call, when Mrs Bedspring telephoned to say that her husband, Spodmore, had been taken over by a spirit. Grogg found him standing on the kitchen table with his trousers round his ankles, singing the German national anthem. The spirit was later identified as vodka.

Villagers are a little worried that the Doctor increasingly trusts Figgy, his Psychic Hamster. Figgy has a wheel in his cage, wired to a board of lights, each of which has a diagnosis. Patients are told to stare at the hamster for three minutes, and then, depending on how fast he runs in the wheel, one light is illuminated. Figgy has identified a headache, arthritis and flu, but doubts were raised last week when elderly Sydney Twitch got a light that was earmarked 'pregnant'. Never one to question Figgy's judgement, Dr Grogg congratulated Sydney and gave him some pamphlets about becoming a mother.

Off record, the Doctor once left some old surgical instruments in his waiting room for children to play with, and we remain impressed that young Razor Trubshaw managed to remove his sister's appendix whilst his mother was being seen for an ingrowing toenail.

Not the Bermuda Triangle

Most of you will know the Bermuda Triangle, but perhaps not the Shawley Nott Parallelogram. The zone covers our ancient stones and the phenomena include disappearances, such as a herd of sheep, several garden gnomes and Enid Thurrox. The sheep were Shawley Nott's famous hyper-intelligent breed, so it's not inconceivable they could have obtained passports, hired a bus, and left the country.

Enid's case was the strangest, as her husband, Theo Thurrox, explains: "She was my second wife, and I told her not to go in the Parallelogram, but she did and she was never seen again. Of course, I was laying a new concrete floor in the basement, so I didn't notice she was missing for some time. I informed the police, so there's nothing suspicious and certainly no need to dig up the floor. It was rather sad because my first wife disappeared in the Parallelogram five years earlier, just as I was laying the patio in the garden, although there's no need to dig that up either."

Strange illuminations have been seen in the zone, but these could be due to the local Pigeon Club putting tiny lights on the feet of its homing pigeons so that they can land in the dark.

Professor Nigel Beeswax, Shawley Nott's resident academic, thinks the Parallelogram phenomena could be due to magnetism. "Magnetic fields exist," he explains, "so I took my research assistant, Raquel, to test my theories. I made a number of different approaches, but sadly there was no magnetism between us whatsoever. In fact, in the end she slapped my face. So now I'm not only looking for a cause for the Parallelogram goings-on, but also a new research assistant. One thing we can say is that whoever originated the Parallelogram theory had no worries about spelling."

Freak Weather

Freak weather conditions are so frequent in Shawley Nott that 'freak' hardly seems the right word. The freak is, in fact, normal, so anything normal would be better described as freak. A gentle breeze can cause serious concern, whereas a light shower of minced beef will barely turn a head. During the past two centuries it has not only rained frogs and tadpoles, but also teaspoons, sultanas, pork pies, underpants and false beards. Records show that in the 14th century the village disappeared in fog for three years. When the fog finally lifted, Mrs Edith Hamstring was surprised to discover that her eldest daughter, Nuria, had a two-year-old son. Despite his father never being identified, 'Foggy' Hamstring lived to be 92 years old.

The only thing it seems not to have rained in Shawley Nott is cats and dogs, although very early the parish records don't clearly explain how Amos D'Arcy was killed by a falling Cocker Spaniel.

Only recently, high winds and floods allowed Mildew Thorpswell to sail his yacht down the High Street, but the elements eventually threw him overboard and he landed in a fine crop of beetroot on an island of allotments. Several fine specimens were squashed, and Mildew found himself marooned in every sense of the word.

2. February

Witchcraft and Fending Off a Vampire with a Spoon

The village school offers evening classes and past successes have included the 'How To..' series: 'How To Avoid Falling In Your Own Cauldron', 'How To Stroke a Werewolf Without Losing Your Arm', and 'How To Fend Off a Vampire with Light Cutlery'. The last of those particularly helped Ethel Fudge when she got caught unawares in her kitchen. In fact, had it not been for her dexterity with a selection of spoons and a whisk we may never have seen her in daylight again.

Witchcraft fills the schedules most terms, with Basic Witchcraft (Mon), Advanced Witchcraft (Tues), Witchcraft with Aero-modelling (tutored by Mr Balsawood, Wed), Witchcraft with Yoga (Thurs), and finally Caring for your Black Cat And Beginners Swedish (Fri). The village's popular annual weekend conference, 'Flying On Your Broom', will return this year and, not before time, will include safety nets. A digital camera link will allow the course to be seen by those still recovering after last year's fiasco.

Off record, the evening course in Ancient Wickerwork has had to be postponed after Shawley Nott's resident expert, Dr Marvin Threadit, accidentally wove himself into his garden fence whilst constructing it.

Séance, Sinatra & Shergar

The Shawley Nott Séance Circle meets once a month, and in their modernist approach we believe they are the first group to try to contact the dead by mobile phone. Last meeting, the phone was in the middle of the table. A majority vote meant the group was trying to contact 'a muscular Roman gladiator', when suddenly the phone started ringing. After several screams of "No, you answer it" and "What rate will it incur?", Madam President took the initiative, only to find it was her husband seeking the whereabouts of the TV remote control.

A few months back they did manage to contact F Sinatra by email, until Mr Sinatra revealed his Christian name was Freddy and he was a young Australian landscape gardener with an interest in bodybuilding. Several Circle members stayed in touch after receiving his photo.

All séances take place in Mrs Napsack's house, where members prefer the room to be quickly plunged into darkness because the curtains and wallpaper clash horrendously. There are frequent knocks, but no latecomers are admitted. The most exciting evening was when elderly Beatrice Snoggin went into a trance, and appeared to contact Shergar, the famous English racehorse kidnapped in 1983. After calling the horse's name, rolling her head from side to side, and speaking in incoherent tones, her friend pointed out that she was diabetic and was actually asking for 'sugar'. A couple of glucose tablets soon saw matters return to normal.

Perhaps the scariest night occurred when the circle asked 'Who is it? Who's there?', only for the door of the room to burst open and a huge white figure appear. "It's me - Mrs Teaspoon," said the figure. "Oh God! Mrs Teaspoon is dead!" cried a séance member. "No I'm not," she replied, "I'm just a bit late and it's snowing heavily."

There have been occasional problems in getting to the séance table after switching the lights off. Mrs Napsack has twice fallen over Ribcage, her faithful whippet, and gone headfirst into her tropical fish tank.

Vegi Yeti

There was a minor crisis recently when a yeti was spotted on the village allotments. Police Constable Willis, the village's local law enforcement officer, asked the allotment owner to describe it, and a slight misunderstanding led to the yeti being recorded as "about 4 yards by 3 yards, with two rows of carrots, a cabbage patch, and a corner section hosting beans".

Despite the confusion, this was not the first report of a yeti in Shawley Nott. Rhubarb Tom, who you might think was nicknamed after his prize allotment exhibit but, in fact, received the title because of his thin face, overly pink complexion and wild expanse of green hair, was the only witness on the previous occasion. The creature was once again in allotment territory, and burst from a fine crop of sprouts. "It had a large shaggy fur coat, thin fleshy legs, and a large mop of ginger hair," Rhubarb Tom explained, "and it was wearing training shoes." His final comment did raise some eyebrows, but it was decided that since many yetis have been tracked by their footprints, the village was obviously home to one of the more intelligent of the species.

Cursed Theatre

Rumour has it that Wilson Maynard-Dinge, who once trod the boards in the West End before retiring to Shawley Nott, placed a curse on all future village theatre productions on his deathbed in 1892, not long after being refused a part in the 1891 Nativity play. As the then director pointed out, the refusal was only because of his role the previous year, when as a Wise Man he had stumbled on stage fuelled by alcohol, and had caused mayhem by commandeering the gold, frankincense, and myrrh. Despite pleas from the other two wise men, he refused to hand over any of the gifts, resulting in an undignified struggle with both Joseph and Mary. As the curtain was closed, Wilson's final action and comment – pushing Joseph over the crib and slurring "These are mine. Get the kid an abacus" – were felt highly inappropriate.

The curse was taken lightly, but lately productions have gone in strange directions. The 1998 attempt at "The Sound of Music" saw the Von Trapp family fail to escape from Austria, whilst the stage version of "Titanic" in 2004, which admittedly was a little ambitious, saw most of the audience rescued by lifeboat. The demands of the special effects caused water restrictions in the village for the following six months. Last year, a printing error on the programme cover proclaimed the performance of Shakespeare's "Omlet".

Our current retired thespians, Ogden Trilby and Vernon Rothschild, host a monthly village ghost walk, but the last word should perhaps be left with the aforementioned Mr Maynard-Dinge: "Give me a beard and I'll be a pirate, give me a cape and I'll be a musketeer; but most of all give me a dress and let me be myself". He was no doubt quite a card for the late Victorian era.

Alien Abduction

Hardly a week goes by without an alien abduction in the village of one sort or another. Apparently aliens are responsible for one current pregnancy, with the 25-year-old in question claiming she was abducted, prodded and probed by creatures that looked like a cross between a giant squid and a wheelie bin. Most villagers, however, suspect Colin. There was a similar case five years ago, but the child shows no alien features whatsoever, and whilst he likes eating beetles, our village child psychologist considers it's just a phase he's going through.

Mrs Dunwoody is still missing and her husband claims she would be of particular interest to any alien species looking to identify human weaknesses, especially regarding the bladder. And the late Mrs Twinsett, of course, always claimed she had been taken aboard a huge ship and woke up next to an alien with long brown ears, a large, wet nose, and sad yet longing eyes. However, whilst this could have been an alien abduction, she could also have been recalling a cruise taken in the 1950s with her spaniel, Mr Smoothy.

Strange Birthday Disasters

Birthday parties seem to encourage odd occurrences in Shawley Nott. There have been one or two calamities in past years, particularly Ginger Pritchard's fifth, when an over-enthusiastic balloon modeller insisted on making extra-large examples of his work, and filled them with helium for added effect. Thankfully four-year-old Daisy Buttercup managed to cling on to her giant poodle until Major Sproates got airborne and plucked her from its paw in his Tiger Moth. Optimistically, Pass the Parcel was delayed until Daisy's return, but sadly her hands were trembling so much that she couldn't hold on to the package.

Ginger's seventh, a few days ago, was reasonably successful, although 'Murder in the Dark' should perhaps have been explained a little more clearly to young Razor Trubshaw. The catering was a little unusual, with two children temporarily getting lost in the Lemon Meringue Pie, whilst two others were attacked by the blancmange. Ginger himself tried to avoid proceedings at one point, but was immediately spotted inside the lime jelly.

3. March

Days of the Living Dead

People frequently rise from the dead in Shawley Nott. A famous case was the village accountant, who died in 1973 and rose again, but a little too rapidly to throw off the tax authorities and he was jailed for six years. The Village Council recorded the whole affair as "gross", a word that was coincidentally mentioned in the accountant's prosecution.

There was a suggestion by Mrs Pipedown that her husband had also risen from the dead, but as he'd been cremated this seemed unlikely. She later confessed that it could easily have been some barbecue ashes caught in a strong breeze. The most startling 'zombies' were spotted by short-sighted Doris Spoonbender, who witnessed two of them 'rising through a portal in the High Street'. She promptly attacked both, but even when the misunderstanding was resolved, the Water Board refused to send any further workmen for more than a month.

Bernard Radish, the village cultural expert, gives a regular talk in the Church Hall about touring the Algarve with his wife Mavis in the 1970s, complete with slides and postcards. His audiences have no connection with the living dead, although as his presentation progresses that fact becomes increasingly difficult to believe.

Vampire Dentist

There is one dental practice in Shawley Nott, and it hasn't helped the village's fight against vampires. With hindsight, when the Village Council selected the new dentist, Dr Seymour Gumm, they were confused by his CV and misread 'experimental', which he is, as 'experienced', which he isn't. Many villagers' teeth have been sharpened, some in the style of a vampire, some in their entirety. Bob 'Squeaky' Bedspring was a victim of the former, although is now a welcome guest at Halloween parties, whereas Enid Twynne was a victim of the latter, giving rise to her nickname of 'Wolfy', which is rather unkind in view of her 85 years. However, on a positive note, during a recent power failure she had no problem consuming raw meat for several days.

The dentist still 'practices', and young Winslow Padding's teeth have recently been on the receiving end of such delicate metalwork that every time he eats a toffee they chime. And, of course, vanity cursed Miss Darling Pout, who asked the dentist for teeth that 'would gleam eternally and draw amazing comments from all who saw them'. Her request was fulfilled when Gumm took them all out, polished them, and put them on a necklace for her.

Witch Class

The village school takes great pride in its academic record, although some of the children's pranks have been a little inexcusable. Not so long ago, Miss Gibbins, a teacher with more than forty years experience, was tied to a chair and dunked in the village pond in a makeshift witch trial. All of the six-year-olds on the nature walk were held accountable, despite trying to justify their behaviour by saying they'd seen her with a broom. (She'd been sweeping the classroom floor at the time.) "She has a moustache" was another excuse, undoubtedly undeniable, but it was felt hereditary misfortune down the female family line was not an indication of guilt in the black arts.

The whole class were made to write on the school blackboard "We must not tie Miss Gibbins to a chair and dunk her in the village pond" one hundred times, although we were unable to identify the party who later removed the word 'not'. Miss Gibbins herself was suspected, as she had an occasional tendency towards thrill-seeking, as Mr. Tussocks, the school caretaker, can vouch. In a fit of passion, Miss Gibbins once pursued him across the school playing fields bearing only a table tennis bat. When Mr Tussocks tried to hide himself in a classroom, the result was two broken desks and an attempted early hibernation by Gerald, the school guinea pig.

A Problem for every Remedy

Herbal remedies in Shawley Nott date from ancient times, but only Mrs Wichess-Brew insists on using them at the moment. Her daffodil syrup remedy for flu doesn't actually cure, but gives the sufferers so many other ailments that the flu is no longer a concern. Other concoctions are bottles of bee's milk and jars of cow honey, although there's a suggestion she loses concentration when preparing labels. For diversification, her ointment to help Malcolm Binderthong's shyness was 'essence of hinge and parrot'. It hasn't worked too well, but at least he's now slightly more willing to open up and talk about the problem. Daphne Doolally put her Wattle & Daub paté on her crackers for months to cure his psychological difficulties, but she still died believing she was Winston Churchill.

Coconut seems to be one of Mrs Wichess-Brew's favourite ingredients, which she uses for butter, milk, oil, shampoo, toothpaste and lip balm. However, her most curious handmade products are her cigarettes, which also have a connection with her coconut product line. After smoking one, she often straps half of a coconut shell to each foot, and canters around her patio pretending to be a horse.

Good Lord! Voodoo Muffins

Hilda Doughmore's Voodoo Muffins are famous throughout Shawley Nott. The muffins are baked to resemble villagers and by accident (or so Hilda says) a muffin of the village mayor burnt during baking, completely incinerating his flamboyant pastry hat. Later that day the mayor, in full regalia, leant forward at the Shawley Nott Embroidery & Resurrection Circle awards dinner. His hat's ostrich feather caught in a candle and the whole lot went up in flames. The Resurrection contingent of the Circle made things worse by bringing his ermine collar back to life. He was lucky to escape with minor burns, a few bites and a tetanus injection. The ermine was later captured near the blancmange.

Coincidentally, the muffin of the mayor also lost its dough moustache as Hilda was lifting it from the oven. On arrival home from hospital, the mayor tried to bite a piece of duct tape in order to repair a cable, but sneezed whilst doing so. His wife managed to tear the tape off his mouth as quickly as possible, but not without some inevitable consequences for the bushy stretch of hair above his upper lip.

Another muffin that Hilda heavily over-baked was of our Italian restaurant owner, who was later found wedged and somewhat blackened in his pizza oven, whilst an excess of icing sugar on a muffin shaped like Mrs Tarmack saw her become the victim of a freak snowstorm in June.

Perhaps the spookiest occurrence was the muffin she made of Miss Flowerhill Sunrise, a villager who is a great believer in Eastern mysticism. For the first time, Hilda actually tried sticking voodoo pins into the muffin, countless times, but with no apparent effect. The following day Miss Sunrise tripped over her hand-woven relaxation rug and fell on her bed of nails.

4. April

Den of IniquiTea

Despite the words 'Cream Teas' sounding identical to the description of Myrtle Sorbet which circulated rather cruelly around her engagement party due to her choice of off-white attire, we do in fact have two little cream tea businesses in the village. Hilda Goodas and Ethel Gold are the two proprietors, and competition is cut throat. New flavours of tea leap off the shelves, particularly the ones that contain frog.

Hilda's last experiment was 'Randylion', made with the small garden flower but professing aphrodisiac qualities, while Ethel countered with 'Mexican Popacuppapetal', which exploded in the mouth. Rumours once spread that the ladies tried to poison each other but the culprit proved to be a bad batch of cream, which both parties had purchased under the influential slogan 'Get Clotted'.

A merger was considered, with the combination of "Goodas Gold" begging to be incorporated. However, the joint venture never got off the ground because of a fundamental difference of opinion about the brewing time of Ceylon Toad, and the failure to agree on a slogan. Hilda wanted "My tea is mighty", whereas Ethel preferred "Our tea is arty". The outcome was a fight, during which both ladies crashed through the front window of the Hilda's tea shop damaging, as the Mayor jested, their "dignitea and popularitea".

Dance like the Devil or Ostrich

Shawley Nott's dances are wild affairs, and the 'Slap and Nudge', which takes place to accordion music, has always been the most popular. Twelve villagers dance in a circle, first slapping their own heads, then the heads of their neighbours. Next, each participant picks up a Great Slapper, which is basically rubber mat on the end of a broomstick, enabling slapping of any participant as long as the circle is maintained. The accordion player then stops for 15 seconds to allow nudging. When he re-starts, anyone not on their feet is disqualified.

Many villagers still remember seeing our most famous performer, Maurice Dancing, but sadly Maurice died in 1983. The Dancing family did their best to wheel him out between 1984 and 1989, but he really lacked any sort of rhythm in those years. His son, Young Maurice, may well continue the tradition when he reaches his sixteenth birthday, and his mother has already sewn bells on his trousers.

In addition to the 'Slap and Nudge', and despite the popularity of the 'Peach Melba' and the 'Plumber's Wrench', the 'Ostrich Strut' is perhaps our best-loved dance, during which villagers, feathered and wearing flippers, swing their legs in strange ways, accompanied by the brass section of the village band. Why it's always the brass section that joins the dance when they should really be playing the music is a mystery. For the climax, the music stops and the band (minus the brass section) shouts 'Strut!' The villager voted the worst Strutter is feathered and flippered for six months.

Off record, Shawley Nott's extraordinary dance and fish tribute – Let's Hake, Cuttle and Sole – is undertaken on the eve of St Haddock's Day.

Headless Horse Horseman – Scary Ghost or a Steed in Need?

The legend of Shawley Nott's Headless Horseman is a little unusual because it's the horse that doesn't have a head, not the man - a sort of Headless Horse Horseman. Many discussions take place as to whether the Horseman really exists, and if so, where does he attach the reins?

Witnesses claim the Horseman lacks the blaze of action associated with other galloping ghosts, and instead appears very cautious, with the horse edging down the High Street one hoof at a time or using the church wall for guidance. Apparently on some occasions the Horseman dismounts and leads to save time.

There is also controversy about whether the rider carries the horse's head under his arm, or whether he's carelessly misplaced it. (We should mention that last week Dozy Prendergast, the only man in the village who doesn't tend his garden, found a severed horse's head in his bed, but the accompanying note – 'Trim your borders' – suggested this was a dispute with a neighbour rather than the solution to a ghostly mystery.) We believe the Headless Horse Horseman must once have been a highwayman, as he sometimes wails 'Stand and deliver!' Unfortunately Frothy Dinsdale, terrified and slightly deaf, misheard the cry as 'Stand in the river' and is now looking to prosecute both the man and his stallion for a new pair of shoes.

Off record, the village also has an Armless Postman and a Gormless Butcher.

The Goats Who Stare at Men

Many goats in Shawley Nott appear to be staring at people. There have been a number of theories put forward for this – they're bored, they're stupid, they're bored and stupid, or possibly they're observing our ways and plan to take over the village sometime next year.

Malcolm Binderthong is convinced they're exercising mind control, as a goat watched him, and he kept an eye on the goat, all the way down the High Street until he accidentally head butted the Post Office door. "But was it just carelessness? Or was the goat influencing my mind? I am not a clumsy man," he stressed at a village Goat Threat meeting. His case was somewhat weakened when he later fumbled his mobile phone into his beer, stepped back in surprise and fell over a coffee table.

Shawley Nott's optician is looking to solve the problem, and has fitted all of the village's fifteen goats with spectacles. "Quite honestly, they had a problem with their vision," he states, "but now they seem much happier, and actually look a little more intellectual." But Deirdre Darkside still has doubts. "Glasses or not, after one stared at me yesterday I felt an urge to have kids," she admits, "and worse than that, my husband's called Billy."

It was pointed out that the goats could be unnerved because young Boris Morris had been feeding them chocolate and moving the animals up and down vigorously, in the hope of that they may produce flavoured milk shake. The matter was left open, although when three goats did escape from their pen, their staring and concentration seemed to focus on a shrubbery. The meeting was closed when the chairman, with his bearded chin and wispy white hair, said goats should be worshipped as they were the most attractive creatures known to man. An appointment has been made for him to see the optician too.

Spirit World, Ghosts, nice Pub and Eel Surprise

The village has a nice pub, The Wicker Man, with many odd features, most of which are attached to the regular clientele.

The pub is haunted, and last month a huge woman, her face and hands covered with green slime and her hair full of a soapy ectoplasm, appeared on the stairs screaming 'Help me! Help me!' The pub emptied, although the 'ghost' proved to be the landlord's wife, having jumped out of the shower after a sachet of Mrs Wichess-Brew's celery and lettuce face gel exploded whilst she was trying to open it. The true ghost appears regularly, and although never seen, it clearly loves the spirit world. Every time it's heard, the pub's best whisky disappears, and the landlord apparently suffers too, waking with a severe headache and a lack of balance.

If the ancient oak beams in the pub could talk, they would boast about witnessing affairs of State in the seventeenth century. The State was represented by the Chancellor of the Exchequer, and the affairs in question were three young dairymaids from Mutton Farm.

Popular pub games include darts, dominos, and eel surprise. The latter takes place late every Wednesday night, when Finny Finnegan puts on rubber gloves, takes an electric eel in each hand from the pub fish tank, and jump-starts anyone who has fallen asleep. There's only been one accident to date, when Finny's attention was distracted and the eels wobbled uncontrollably. The unfortunate victim had a number of gold and silver fillings, and as the eels connected with his lips the shock soldered his teeth together. He complained in the strongest possible terms "Hmmm mmmm hmm mmmm!"

Off record, Exotic Spider Racing on takes place every Tuesday, although last week Norman's Giant Hairy Brazilian Blue was banned for cocooning one of the bar staff.

5. May

Fete and fortune

Every May the Shawley Nott Village Fete takes place, a day of strange traditions and even stranger homemade preserves. Our raffle has been operating for countless years, and was no doubt started by a budding entrepreneur – the first (and only) prize is ten free tickets for next year's draw.

The 'What's Hilda Knitting?' competition always attracts great interest, and speed-knitter Hilda last year skillfully concealed that she was knitting a Gatling gun until almost her last stitch. Incredibly, it was fully functional in a handicraft sense, and after loading it with a cartridge Hilda proceeded to pepper the cake stall with buttons. Just before that revelation, the Shawley Nott football team had lost the tug-of-war to the Embroidery Circle, and young Colin had again won the three-legged race, not least because he's one of only four children in the village who don't require a partner.

Clown, vampire and animal designs tend to do well in the Face Painting competition, although it's perhaps best not to mention the occasion when 78-year-old Doris Throttlegate triumphed as a turn-of-the-century French prostitute. Her first comment, "What Face Painting competition?", drew a nervous silence from the crowd.

The Brotherhood of the Headless Chicken

Shawley Nott has its own secret Brotherhood, which meets in the cemetery whenever there's a full moon. The maximum membership is seven, which many people think is because of the mysterious properties of the number, but it's actually because the group only possesses seven black robes. It's believed the Brotherhood of the Headless Chicken was started by one of Lord Harbinger's ancestors (see January), who in trying to defend the village from invaders frankly just panicked and ran around a lot.

Admission is by 'dead men's shoes', so whenever anyone passes away in the village there's always a scuffle in front of their wardrobe during the wake. Each member of the Brotherhood has a Grand Master title, such as Grand Master Claw, Grand Master Pointy Beak, or Grand Master Feathered Rear. The black robes are huge affairs, with enormous hoods and such starched cloth that they stand up on their own. One dark night Grand Master Crippled Wing was asked a question and silence provoked the other six members to look into his robe, only to discover he'd gone home.

The objective of the Brotherhood is to embrace the concept of panic on the basis that no problem is too great as long as you can lose your head in looking to solve it. Every meeting culminates with the same dramatic Q&As:

Grand Master Claw: We are a Brotherhood! Are we smart?

Other members: (together, enthusiastically) No, we're clueless!

Grand Master Claw: Are we brave?

Other members: (enthusiastically) No, we're spineless!

Grand Master Claw: And are we tigers?

Other members: No, we're Headless Chickens!

All seven then run around in the cemetery, clucking and waving their hands in the air. In the darkness and with the hoods it's not unusual for them to fall over a tombstone, and Grand Master Pointy Beak was once knocked unconscious by Wallace Snoot (1745-1809), which was a considerable achievement for a man who's been dead for more than 200 years.

Off record, there is no connection between the Brotherhood and the Shawley Nott Eternal Youth Sisterhood, or the Shawley Nott Cub Scouts, even though all three groups organize summer camping trips.

Plague Alert – Ducks, Kippers, Giant Wood Lice

Shawley Nott village plagues have included spiders, mice, ducks, liquorice, fleas, fruit bats, gnomes, marbles, boils and door-to-door fancy dress salesmen. The salesman were the worst, and when they were found to be charging outrageous prices for their costumes they were chased down the High Street by their customers, who included Napoleon, Batman, Robin Hood, the Archbishop of Canterbury and a furious Elton John. The last ten years have also seen us endure a flock of hammers, an influx of pudding mix, an outbreak of kippers, and three giant wood lice that ate the bus shelter.

The Village Council appointed an official Plague Consultant but for extortionate fees he produced a 600 page document suggesting that plagues may, or may not, be tax deductible. In the end, Hamish MacMcDuggiedougall volunteered to examine Old Tweezer's Book of Fears, the most ancient volume in the village library. His conclusions have been that September will bring sporrans, October will see moths, and in November we can expect 'evil, wide-eyed beasts dressed in chiffon to leap from time-travel booths and steal our minds'. Just after proclaiming his research, Hamish saw Ethel Fudge exit the village telephone box, dressed up for her bingo night, and attacked her screaming "They've arrived! They've arrived!" We managed to get him off her on the grounds that it wasn't yet November, although Ethel later admitted that her entire wardrobe was chiffon. Happily, she's agreed to stay indoors throughout the autumn and winter.

Off record, the village was once inundated with ventriloquist dolls; just the dolls, not their human operators, which wasn't too worrying until they started speaking.

Witchcraft at School

Last week one Shawley Nott youngster chalked a five-pointed star in the playground because he'd had Webster, his pet tarantula, confiscated during a surprise desk search. The star was thought harmless until Norma Cauldron hopped into it and promptly changed into a toad. Efforts are being made to change her back, but apparently she's doing much better in her swimming lessons and also, surprisingly, in maths.

The school has always had problems. In 1927, one teacher decided to play 'Hide and Seek' with class 2B, none of whom were ever seen again. As the then headmaster said, "Either we have a tragedy, or possibly the most talented class for this game that the world has ever known." In the early 70s, Mr Tibbett's nature class was told to press wild flowers (an old hobby whereby nature is preserved by pressing specimens in the pages of a heavy book) and whilst most of the class stuck to flora, one or two pressed insects or cakes, and Wilma Hartless even tried to press her best friend. The *pièce de résistance* however came from Solly Beckerstein, who opened a volume of the Encyclopedia Britannica to reveal Mrs. Spoonbender's rather one-dimensional chihuahua. Solly was severely reprimanded and since a duck was discovered in his school bag the same afternoon the ticking off was only just in time. The chihuahua was resuscitated, although after the incident Mrs Spoonbender only had to open her front door a fraction to let him in.

Incidentally, witchcraft has at last been removed from the timetable, although the school caretaker still has a head like a large piece of cheese.

The World's Worst Hypnotist

The village hypnotist did his annual show again this year, but last year's fiasco has yet to be forgotten. On that occasion, villager Nugent Throbb volunteered for the hypnotist's ten minute 'Stop Smoking Now' therapy. Sure enough, the treatment worked, but primarily because Nugent now believes he's a lawnmower. "It was easier to put up with his smoking than to watch him try to hover back and forth over the lawn every night," declares his wife.

The hypnotist had great fun on stage by making one resident believe he was a tom cat. This went quite well when the victim licked his hands and cleaned behind his ears, but there was a major incident on his way home when he stole some milk from the grocery shop. As PC Willis approached him, the unfortunate victim arched his back and spat.

"All the hypnotist's efforts to de-hypnotize him have failed miserably," complains his mother, "I had to cuff him round the ear recently for sharpening his nails on the leg of the kitchen table."

The most depressing case is Shawley Nott's door-to-door cleaningware salesman, who was hypnotized into believing he was an alien. "I've suffered," he says, "because sometimes when people answer their door I say 'Cleaning products?' but sometimes I clamp my hand on their head and say 'I've come to steal your mind'. Believe me, you don't sell much floor polish after that."

Sadly, attempts to de-hypnotize Maurice Tipple from being a stork have come to a temporary halt as he's nesting on top of a telephone post.

6. June

The Oak that Spoke – Witchcraft, Rituals and Penguins

The history of Shawley Nott's ancient oak tree is remarkable - attempted hangings, witchcraft, naked dancing and midnight rituals - and those only in the last two months. There is a rumour that the tree whispers instructions, although interpreting the rustle of the leaves is open to question. 'Shop at Elsie's fantastic village store for unbeatable prices' was a regular message until a hidden speaker was found in the upper branches, whilst mysterious one-offs include 'Make a pineapple soufflé', 'Buy a deckchair' and 'Tell Feldstein his penguin has perished'.

The tree was famous in the 1700s for a family of dancing squirrels, and the tip of its shadow is said to pinpoint buried treasure. This might have been satisfactory on bare land three centuries ago, but it now leads to intrusions through Mrs Tinderbox's front window and unauthorised digging in her lounge.

Just before Christmas several villagers fled after hearing the tree cry "Help me!" and "I'm bleeding!" PC Willis investigated the next day, and found old Mr Bleckinsop in a nearby ditch, having fallen off his bike. As he was stretchered into the ambulance he complained about neglect, then the cold breeze, before finally asking "Has the seat been ripped out of my pants?"

In Spring, all the village youngsters dance around the oak, then run towards the trunk and viciously prod each other.

Rather embarrassingly, the dance is known locally as doing the oaky-pokey.

Off record, we can reveal that in the sixteenth century Kay Strapper, a woman of rather easy virtue, used to sell her favours under the tree, with no offer ever declined. She became known locally as Oak Kay.

How To Defeat A Vampire With A Spoon

The following is a curious transcript of Ethel Fudge's report about how she vanquished a vampire with a spoon. She spoke at the Village Institute but was somewhat heckled by old Mrs Barnacle, who is a little deaf and never one to mince her words:

Ethel: Well, I was in the kitchen, thinking about whether to make some fresh soup or whether to take tinned instead.

Mrs Barnacle: (loudly) Don't worry. I do that regularly.

Ethel: Do what, dear?

Mrs Barnacle: (loudly) Break wind in bed.

(General comments of "What?", "She said 'take tinned instead' you fool" and "Get on with it.")

Ethel (visibly shaken): So I turned round and there he stood. A vampire!

(Gasps of "No!", "Whatever next!" and "Do vampires like soup?")

Ethel: (continuing) Well, his face was as white as a meringue, his teeth as long and sharp as two white asparagus tips and his eyes were as red as glacé cherries.

Mrs Barnacle: (aside) I suddenly feel peckish.

(General cries of "Never mind her, what did you do?")

Ethel: (continuing again) Without a moment's hesitation I picked up a spoon and hit him; three inches above the nose, with the convex part facing down. If you get it just right you hear a wonderful 'donk'. He quickly clutched his head and went 'Oooooooh!'

(General cheers of "Oooooh!", "Bravo!", and "Who'd have thought it! A spoon!")

Ethel: So then the commotion brought my husband in from the garden, and fortunately he thrust a huge fence post through the vampire's chest. That's it really.

(Disappointed comments of "Did she say a fence post?", "That's an anti-climax", and "Was that it with the spoon?")

Ethel: Of course, when the vampire turned to dust, we both grinned.

Mrs Barnacle: (loudly, to other members): Did she say they broke wind?

(General closing comments of "No dear", "She said 'both grinned' you fool" and "Someone take her home.")

So, just for clarity, it appears that to defeat a vampire you need a spoon, plus a large fence post.

Off record, Mrs Barnacle's hearing deficiency is becoming a problem and last week she complained aloud when she couldn't find her seat in church. "You've a place by the third pew," shouted the vicar. "You've a face like a turd stew too," she answered, and poked him in the eye with her stick.

Not Sweeney Todd – Shawley Nott's Demon Barber

Fleet Street had Sweeney Todd as its demon barber, whilst in the eighteenth century Shawley Nott had Teeny Bod, who at just one metre tall must have been the shortest barber in England. History suggests he only cut one throat, which happened whilst he was shaving the baker - Teeny sneezed violently, toppled off his podium, and had the misfortune to see the baker's head roll across the floor. The only compensation was that he'd already styled the hair so he was able to use the head as a window display for almost three months.

Teeny's talent was for sideburns, which he would cut, curl, dye and perm. His favourite design was to style each into the face of a Yorkshire terrier, which looked remarkable, especially on women.

He used the hair from his clients to make dolls for the village children, but his doll-making skills left a lot to be desired. The children thought about building a small dolls' house to keep their new gifts in, but after studying the figures they decided a zoo would be more suitable.

He is believed to be one of the first people to try a hair transplant, securing the hair he'd cut to those in need by his own special paste made of ground nuts and wood chippings. Sir Frinton Nibbly died with his chest hair 'as thick as an impenetrable forest', and just before he was buried a family of squirrels were found to be living in it. Sir Frinton's wife, Lady Harriet, spoke of undergoing several transplants, but never appeared to change her looks. However, when Sir Frinton's house caught fire and she had to lift her skirts to jump from a window, she was said to have revealed 'legs with a coat like a grizzly bear'.

Teeny Bod died after falling into huge dish of soapy shaving cream. It took a long time to remove his corpse, as every time someone tried he slipped through their hands and fired round the dish like a torpedo.

What Lurks in the Crypt – Werewolf or What?

A strange growling can often be heard from the church crypt and opinion is divided as to whether the vicar is really a werewolf, or the crypt hides a hideous monster. The lower part has been flooded for many years, so the case has been made for an alligator or a very large rabbit with scuba gear. Long scratch marks on the crypt door are inconclusive.

Suspicion was raised about the werewolf theory recently when several villagers took their pet dogs to the vicar's Sunday service. They all started howling uncontrollably, which set the dogs off too. However, since it happened a few seconds after the church choir started to sing, the matter remains open.

Whatever is in the crypt, it needs feeding and the vicar buys enough raw meat to make three casseroles a day. Even though the quality of meat from our butcher has diminished of late Miss Tartlebaum, our organist, thinks the vicar could be cooking it, slicing it up, and using it to mend the church roof.

If it is an alligator, there could clearly be an underground link between the crypt and Mr & Mrs Smitten's garden pond, and might explain why only Mr Smitten's left leg was discovered after he went out to feed the goldfish.

Professor Nigel Beeswax has examined the evidence, and declared "We have a beast that can live in and out of water, makes noises, and is intelligent enough to scratch the crypt doors in an effort to escape. Quite obviously, it's a dolphin with a chisel. And the vicar, therefore, must be eating three casseroles a day."

Off record, late Mr Scarsmore was a known werewolf, which was odd because he was also a vegetarian. On a full moon, he would go out and savagely consume beansprouts.

Gypsy Curse and the Featherless Chicken

A gypsy curse is believed to have been placed on the pitch of Shawley Nott soccer club, as before the team's first fixture a woman was seen in the centre circle, mumbling incoherently. She had wild ginger hair, brightly coloured clothes, excessive make up, and was dragging a goat. Of course, she could have been a curse-placing gypsy, but frankly that description fits quite a number of villagers.

Shawley Nott FC's colours are meant to be white, but it often depends on what other clothing Enid Cloggs puts in her washing machine with the club kit. Unfortunately, she has a favourite red blouse, which means the team often plays in pink.

Perhaps the most frustrating moment in the team's 56 year run of bad luck was in 1992-93, when Shawley Nott were ahead two goals to one after 85 minutes, but then game had to be abandoned because the referee was attacked by Marvin, the village's vicious featherless chicken. We believe the referee's wiry brown hair, which seemed to have been thrown randomly on the top of his head, may have been seen as a nesting opportunity. Some of the players were inconsolable, and our centre half still has to fight back the tears when he sets eyes on his Christmas turkey. The re-match was lost 6-1.

Marvin still roams the village looking for trouble, and has attacked the village ducks, Miss Cartwright's feathered hat, and Mr Kowalski's antique set of quill pens. We referred Marvin to the village psychologist, who diagnosed 'plume envy'. Lord Harbinger only thought it fair to try to feather him (Marvin, not the psychologist), but unfortunately he mis-timed his barrel of glue and feathers, and caught Beryl Shipyard with the full load. Marvin immediately spotted her, and we've never seen Beryl run so fast as when trying to escape his attention. Given her unexpected feathering and arm-flapping on two occasions she actually took off.

Off record, during one game last season, a village gypsy was caught trying to sell Lucky Heather to the small crowd along the edge of the pitch, but Heather's mother found out and was furious.

38

7. July

The Twiggy Monster & St Gwynneth

In addition to Shawley Nott's fete (see May), there is also an annual fiesta, and the good news is that this year there were no fatalities. The Egg & Spoon race was actually won by an egg, and Mrs Pipedown won Best Resuscitation Attempt for her efforts on Jacob Fizzleton (1698-1742). The schedule this year was as follows:

10.00 Blasting of the Gnomes
11.00 Herb Cloggs & His Synchronized Dancing Donkey Troupe
12.00 Light Buffet
1.00 Archery Practice
2.00 Dressing of wounds
3.00 Battle the Twiggy Monster
4.00 Homage to St Gwynneth
5.00 Slaughter of The Infected

Rhubarb Tom (see February) volunteered to be this year's Twiggy Monster, a tradition for which an individual is covered in branches and runs out of the woods to terrify the kids. The children have to get a twig from the monster to avoid being stained green in Miss Fungalmoss's cauldron. Most just use their hands, but Rhubarb Tom panicked a little when Razor Trubshaw powered up his concealed chainsaw.

St Gwynneth, of course, is Shawley Nott's patron saint. Little is known about her, although it appears she sacrificed herself to a party of Vikings who were about to ransack the village, oddly enough in 1925. Some villagers believe she sacrificed herself rather too easily, particularly as she is recorded as striding back down the High Street wearing a horned helmet, caribou leather boots and a broad grin. One of the villagers' favourite cakes during the celebration is called the 'St Gwynneth', which is basically a tart that can cater for several people.

The gold medal for Most Unusual Pet went to Beatrice Minty for her talking pineapple, and the Archery Practice followed by the Dressing of Wounds proved such a strain that next year the targets will be moved well away from the tea and coffee area.

Paranormal Investigations

Shawley Nott's most infamous ghost-hunter is Colonel Gregory Isberg-Lettis, a part-Norwegian ex-army man. During the Vicrorian era, barely a night went by without him, armed with a crossbow, proudly marching the streets. One mill worker was most understanding when he surprised the Colonel late one evening. "I should've washed all this flour off me," the worker said, pale-faced and trembling, as he pulled two arrows from his backside. The Colonel was eventually made to relinquish the weapon after narrowly missing 'a huge white beast from Hell, ready to pounce from the church wall'. Nibbsy, the baker's overfed Persian cat, never knew how lucky she was.

Nowadays we have regular paranormal investigations, most recently in Lord Harbinger of Doom's wine cellar. Two students arrived with electrodes, probes and sound equipment, and confidently confirmed "If there's anything down there, we'll find it". They stayed in the cellar all night, but only managed to locate Lord Harbinger's vintage claret. When they came out the following morning, their sound recording contained phrases like "Let's open this one", "What happens if I probe this area" and a lot of giggling. They greeted Lord Harbinger by saying, "We love you; you're our best friend" and "Do you have an aspirin?"

"My vintage claret has disappeared!" he fumed.

"Paranormal phenomena at last!" yelled one of the investigators, and then fell over.

A previous paranormal investigation was undertaken in the part-flooded church crypt, to investigate the presence there. Theories included an alligator or a rabbit with diving equipment (see June). "My high-tech, multi-frequency, state-of-the-art sound recording equipment definitely picked something up," explained the investigator. When he switched on his tape, a voice could be clearly heard: "Anyone available to pick up Mrs Fuzzard at number 23 Hornsdale Drive and take her to the clinic?" "Yeah I'm close by Charlie. Should be there in five."

Crop Circle Watch Group

The following interview took place with Nora Cobb, president of the Shawley Nott Crop Circle Watch Group:

Interviewer: Nora, how many crop circles have you seen around the village?

Nora: None.

Interviewer: And how many haven't you seen?

Nora: We suspect hundreds. Don't forget, there are only three of us, and lots of fields. Of course, our former member Elgin Tassocks spread himself a little too thinly over one particular area.

Interviewer: He believed it was especially suspicious?

Nora: No, unfortunately he fell in a threshing machine.

Interviewer: You must miss him a lot.

Nora: I should say so - he was the only person who had a pair of binoculars. So now it's just me, Betty and Harold.

Interviewer: What do you think the crop circles that you haven't seen are trying to tell us?

Nora: We believe they are landing sites for Flying Saucers. Circles and saucers are the same shape, after all.

Interviewer: But what if you found a square one?

Nora: You mean a crop square? Don't be ridiculous. Saucers are round; the only square thing in my kitchen is a Pyrex casserole dish. I don't think anyone has heard of aliens in a Flying Pyrex Casserole Dish. It just doesn't make sense.

Interviewer: Do you think the crop circles you haven't seen could have been made by other means?

Nora: We did try to roll Betty in a circle one dark night, just to see the result, but we lost her on a small gradient and she rolled several yards downhill into a drainage ditch. Interestingly though, her route looked as though it was a runway, and Harold suggested we play some music, like in that famous film, to encourage the aliens to land. He had his piano accordion with him, but he stopped after about 45 seconds.

Interviewer: Aliens arrived?

Nora: No. Betty struggled back from the ditch and said that if Harold continued making such a frightful noise, aliens might attack him. And if they didn't, she certainly would.

Interviewer: Finally, do you think the weather is influential?

Nora: Absolutely. We don't go if it's raining.

Nora, Betty and Harold's pamphlet, '20 Years Of Not Finding Crop Circles' is available from the village shop.

Off record, one extremely windy day a local farmer noticed a 'crop shadow' - a dark square on his wheat that was rapidly getting bigger and bigger. He quickly went to investigate, and a few seconds later he was flattened by a large sheet of roofing felt.

The Water Diviner and the Phantom Owl

Rod is Shawley Nott's water-diviner. He uses two L-shaped rods, because a Y-shaped one once sprung upright and became wedged in his left nostril. Rod rushed to Dr Grogg (see January), worried that he might have water on the brain, but the doctor just gave him a tap on the head. The tap displaced it, and it's an endorsement of Rod's talent that he was still clinging to it as he flew across the room straight into the doctor's fish tank.

He is currently testing different divining techniques, substituting his rods with two herring. Holding one fish in each hand, his idea is that they will cross when above a water source. That theory remains open, but he has proved that one man with two herrings is no match for five large seagulls.

His divining recently led him to the beer barrels in our pub, 'The Wicker Man', which caused heated discussions about what the landlord might have done to the beer. The landlord was furious, and Rod again had to go to Dr Grogg, this time to have a herring removed. He continues to write a local column called 'Simply Divine' for the village magazine.

Having commented about seagulls, a mention should also be made about the village's Phantom Owl, a huge ghostly white bird. One dark night it flatly refused to give up on Lord Harbinger's moustache, which it must have mistaken for a field mouse. It drew a small amount of blood, and we think Lord Harbinger may have been infected with Owl Tendency by the way he now eats a slice of bacon. (He holds one end in his hand and pulls at the other with his teeth.) He also squats on the edge of his dining table, says 'twit-twoo', widens his eyes, and scans the floor for movement. However, his maid claims he's done that since he was six years old.

Owl Tendency seems fairly prevalent in Shawley Nott, as Mrs Bedspring was recently found nesting in a barn.

Transylvanian Adventures

Many English towns are twinned with European ones for cultural purposes, but Shawley Nott is inexplicably linked to a village in Transylvania. There have been exchanges – we sent them some of our local cheese, and this month they sent us some beautiful sealed coffins. Major Sproates immediately got to work with his crowbar, but each time a lid was forced off the mannequin inside turned to dust. The Major thought that perhaps our cheese didn't agree with them, so in future we're going to send some of Miss Tartlebaum's Lavender and Toad body lotion, which might provide them with some much-needed moisture. One of the coffins refused to open, and come darkness a voice from inside was heard mumbling "I don't believe this. Halfway across Europe and the lid's stuck."

A one-page tourist guide came with the coffins, but there were only two headings – 'Nightlife' and 'After Dark'. "We haven't much experience with tourists," it read, "but they're really something we'd like to get our teeth into."

In 1975 three Shawley Nott residents made a trip to the Transylvanian village, and we'd almost given up on them until a letter and photo arrived last Christmas. They all looked a bit pale, but not a day older than when they left. The letter explained that a taxi driver, who had lost his upper lip, took them to the edge of the village but refused to go further. He kept pointing and saying "Umpires, umpires", even though none of the locals proved to be keen on playing cricket or refereeing tennis.

The last words belong to Major Sproates: "Frankly," he says, "I wish we'd got Düsseldorf."

8. August

Ghost Train - Going, Going, Gone

The travelling fairground visits the village every August, and it's always pleasant to meet villagers who were enticed to join it the previous year. Many of us blame the fortune-teller with her entrancing brown eyes and seductive voice, who hands out fortune-telling cards showing only a date, a time and her caravan number.

Only three individuals vanished on the Ghost Train last time, although that does bring the number to the twenty-seven in total. One small consolation is that Gregor, the ghost train owner, always gives relatives a partial refund as tickets are sold on a round trip basis. The worst year was 1987, when six villagers got on the train and it became stuck on 'auto'. On completion of the first circuit, all six shouted "There's a..." before rapidly disappearing through the wooden doors for a second time. When the train came round again, the five passengers screamed the word "big..", and the following occasion the four managed to yell "vicious...". The three who appeared a fourth time added "hairy", and on the next appearance "evil" was screamed by the remaining two. When the carriages rolled past the sixth time the single occupant was clearly too traumatized to comment. At least we can confirm that the ride conceals a big vicious hairy evil something.

Gregor was asked what he thought the big vicious hairy evil thing was, but he just shrugged his shoulders and replied "peckish".

It may appear that the Ghost Train is the scariest ride, but we believe that honour goes to the Helter Skelter, where the slide finishes half way down the tower.

Off record, due to a slight miscalculation, Stanislav Boom, the fairground's human cannonball, is still wedged in the brickwork halfway up the village church tower.

All The Fear of the Fair

Continuing our fairground exploits (see previous entry – Ghost Train), the most exciting option is probably the Fun Fair Guillotine, operated by Monsieur Claude, who has to flick a switch to prevent his apparatus slicing a volunteer's head off. If Claude asks his victim "Are you ready?" then it's going to be great fun. However, last year he surprisingly shouted "Are you having an affair with my wife?" after which the victim's desperate apologetic screams were silenced with a shocking reality.

The 'Hook-a-Duck' challenge proved trickier than normal and nine-year-old Phyllis Truncheon failed with a particularly vicious mallard.

Short-sighted Reg Muscle brought the hammer-and-bell 'Test Your Strength' machine to a very early end when he struck the operator and drove him six inches into the ground. Die-hard Reg insisted on trying again, but in an effort to feign his success the panic-stricken operator shouted 'Ding! Ding!" Unfortunately Reg took his cue from the source of the noise, and struck the operator again. This time he was driven so deep that the fairground master quickly improvised and billed him as 'The Incredible Talking Head'.

A small pink ghoul howled round the fair for several minutes, until it was identified as Ginger Pritchard, who'd been standing close to the candy floss machine when it unexpectedly exploded. His father, always entrepreneurial, immediately stood Ginger on a podium, gave passers-by a small stick, told them to hold it towards his son, and whirled him round for twenty pence a time.

Museum of the Strange

The Shawley Nott Museum of the Strange was founded by Captain Thrasher to store the curiosities he brought back from his nineteenth-century travels. The prize exhibit is a stuffed Fnump bird, now extinct. It was an unusual species because it only had one wing, which meant it was extremely good at circling prey but awful at going in for the kill. Its name may relate to the impact it made when missing a field mouse, for example.

A series of shrunken heads is also on show. People tend to think these originate from primitive societies, but they're actually the work of the last museum caretaker, a strict disciplinarian, who carried out the practice on anyone who put their fingers on the glass display cases. It seems quite sordid, but it does make the museum unique in having a visitors' cabinet as well as a visitors' book.

Mrs Crumple, better known as Witchy Crumple, donated her collection of black magic artefacts, which include dried toads, spiders, woolly undergarments, finger nails, and a series of German techno-pop CDs.

Traditional folk costumes are in room four, so it's recommended that visitors go direct from room three to five in order to avoid them. Our temporary exhibition, 'Spirit Possession of Everyday Objects' has closed because the frying pan won't let anyone in.

The Supernatural section is perhaps the best, although chaos reigned for several hours last month when someone removed the wooden stake from the ribcage of the skeleton. A terrifying vampire materialised, and elderly receptionist Miss

Deekins had almost as much trouble vanquishing him as getting him to pay for a ticket. The vampire tried to bite her, but she promptly removed her own teeth, clasped them in her hand, and bit him first.

The fee, by the way, is £1.50 to get in, and £2.75 to get out.

Poltergeists, Portals and a String Vest

The reputations of poltergeists in Shawley Nott aren't all bad, and in fact Nellie Bounce was happy with hers for several years. She was never one for cleaning, and the poltergeist's activity often left her house in a better state than she did. "Also, I could talk to it about knitting," she says. The poltergeist is believed to be the first ever to leave a house of its own accord.

Despite their noise and tantrums, villagers have found that poltergeists can be domesticated. "Mine likes cheese and plums," explains Mrs Wovenquilt, "and I've also trained it to do my ironing. I've called it Brian, and the only problem is that it causes a strange crackling on my TV set."

Of course, there have been violent episodes. Cyril and Mildred Snupple found theirs most demanding, and on one occasion it tried to drag Mildred to 'the other side'. "A portal opened in the back of the closet," explains Mildred nervously, "I was clinging to a piece of string from one of Cyril's vests. As it unravelled, I was going further and further into the poltergeist's lair. Luckily, Cyril's a big man, so before it unravelled completely I managed to pull myself back and smack the poltergeist with a shoe. Cyril just sat on the bed and did nothing."

"Although you could say I had a vested interest," Cyril laughs, before Mildred smacks him with a shoe too.

The vicar's definition of a poltergeist as a 'restless spirit' doesn't receive much support. "My brother had a restless spirit," says Mildred, "so he went backpacking. It didn't give him an excuse to drag me into a fiery underworld." The portal, however, has proved useful, as they now open the door in winter for a little extra heat, and the fire and flames have enabled Cyril to grill toast on an extra long fork from his bed.

Off record, we think one poltergeist was recently caught on security video in the village shop, sucking a bag of frozen peas. But the video was somewhat blurry, so it could be that Mr Sneggins has succumbed to his fetish again.

The Thrill of the Honk

There are many curious customs in Shawley Nott, one of which is 'Honking the Midget'. This originated in Tudor times, when the shortest man in the village had to run down the High Street whilst all other villagers pursued him and tried to blast their horns in his ears. Clearly, chasing a midget is no longer politically correct, so Dimforth Spasm, who is 5 feet 8 inches tall, has been 'volunteer midget' for the last twenty years. His answer to most questions about the event is 'What?'

The current trend is to use clown-style horns, with a rubber ball attached to a brass trumpet, but this year one competitor managed to manipulate a ship's fog horn onto a trolley, and blasted it alongside poor Mr Spasm. The shock blew him through the baker's shop window. The current record of 123 honks in the one hundred yard pursuit is held by Puffer Watkins.

The second tradition is burning a virgin at the stake, which appears to have originated for fun. Of course, this is no longer politically correct either, and even if it was the village may well be struggling to find eligible parties. So nowadays a steak is burnt in front of a virgin, a nice twist on the affair, even though there were one or two very unkind comments about 19-year-old Daphne Polltwanger as the meat was cooked in front of her last year.

The 25th August is the day that anyone waiting in our gents hairdressers is chased by a party of masked villagers carrying blow torches. This was adopted three years ago, and is known as our annual Barber Queue Grill.

9. September

Mad Scientist

Professor Osmond Cartoid is Shawley Nott's resident mad scientist, and can often be seen wandering the streets in his white coat, holding a large jar containing an odd creature up to the sky and mumbling 'Why has it died again?'
He has a slight obsession with trying to breathe life back into the dead and once tried to resuscitate Sandra, the village barmaid, which distressed her considerably because she was standing in the queue at the Post Office at the time.

Anyone who glares through the Professor's lab window can see a number of glass containers with peculiar species, all labelled in Cartoid's unique way – 'Almost', 'Not Quite', or 'Too Many Ears'. The scariest one is labelled 'Pickled Onions', but we suspect that's connected to his dietary preferences rather than a failed experiment.

His famous thesis, entitled 'Facial Hair in the Evolution of Fish', was widely discredited, although the stuffed bearded salmon that stands on his mantelpiece seems real enough. The Professor's lab couch is surrounded by leads, wires, belts and electrodes, and oddly so is his bed.

Spanning his garden gate, a large metal sign initially read 'For a scientist there's nothing better than a first-class proof'. Unfortunately the 'r' in 'proof' fell off two years ago, although he hasn't noticed and nobody has the heart to tell him.

It was suspected that Osmond had created a monster after the last electrical storm. A naked man ran screaming down the High Street with a bolt through his neck, his hair was full of wallpaper glue and with a curtain rail separating his knees.

However, it later proved to be Jack Pastey, having had a rather aggressive tiff with his wife about redecorating the lounge.

Murderous and Evil Bakers

The village bakery has been associated with supernatural occurrences since 1692, when a batch of infected yeast enabled most residents in the village to levitate. Much to everyone's relief, not least the village shoemaker, it only lasted about a week. "My trade relies on people keeping their feet on the ground," the shoemaker complained at the time from just under his shop ceiling.

Mad Beryl Baguette married three consecutive village bakers in the late 1800s, and murdered each of them. She clearly made use of the bakery facilities as the causes of death were recorded as baked, whisked and waffled. She met with an unfortunate end, as in a struggle to avoid the authorities she fell in a vat of trifle sherry, climbed out, staggered too near the oven fire and flambéed herself.

In 1938, the baker's wife fell in love with her work so much that she eloped with a chocolate éclair.

The current baker is again dabbling with supernatural affairs, but his results are a little worrying. Mrs Wovenquilt had a very pleasant chat with a doughnut when in the shop last Tuesday, but on Wednesday Ethel Fudge was set on by a gang of gingerbread men. Fortunately, the self-raising flour got up and defended her.

The baker is always looking to extend his alternate world theory and last weekend decided the Upside Down Cake was actually the right way up. He concluded that everything else, including the shop, was wrong. His efforts to correct the matter caused chaos, not least trying to nail the shop counter to the ceiling.

Not Quite a Freak Show

After the travelling fairground (see August), the Freak Show usually arrives in the village, although lately the exhibits have left a little to be desired. Anyone impressed by the bearded lady clearly hasn't met the mayor's wife and frankly an attraction called 'The Two-armed Man' was clutching at straws with both of them.

'The Three Twins' were obviously triplets, and a spectacular performance called The Incredible Growing Tortoise was exposed as a tortoise/giant turtle substitution, with the only 'incredible' factor, in view of the species, being the relatively quick behind-the-curtain change.

It wasn't always so disappointing. At the turn of the century, there was a baboon that could play the violin and a chameleon that had lost its ability to change colour. The latter may not sound freakish, but it had been taught to quick-knit itself an appropriately toned sweater.

A famous animal attraction in 1888 was called 'What Is It?' The owner said he would name the creature based on votes cast by visitors. Was it a gorilla? Could it be lizard? With a 92% majority it was called 'We have no idea'. For reasons unknown the remaining 8% opted for 'Norman'.

Finally, many villagers' illusions were shattered by the Mermaid, whose delicate image was harmed when the stage curtains opened too soon and she was seen zipping up her tail whilst smoking a cigar.

Witchy Crumple's Curse Course

Witchy Crumple runs a Curse Course in the village for five lucky individuals every September, but had endless problems last year. Her concentration was erratic and by the third day two students had a face like a hedgehog, one had a left leg like a piece of rhubarb, and the other two were stick insects.

"I got a bit confused after my hat fell in the cauldron," Witchy explains, "and I couldn't remember one particular word. I asked the students 'what's that thing that starts with a bee and is all sticky?' And they replied 'bubble gum'. Of course, bubble gum turned two to stick insects. The word I was looking for was 'honey'."

"There was a similar incident two years ago during cauldron training," she continues. "Instead of saying 'Boil her a nasty curse', I accidentally said 'Curse her with nasty boils', a mistake that really put an end to Cynthia Brimstone's social life. But I didn't make the biggest error, which should be attributed to young Algy Sopwell. He should have said 'A pea I add to live forever', but under stress he shouted 'A liver I add to pee forever', and he hasn't been out of the bathroom since."

Witchy thinks nerves can play a devastating role, but ingredients and sequencing are critical. "One student had to squeeze in a lemon, then lick a giant aubergine. Unfortunately, she licked the lemon, winced, panicked, and tried to squeeze in the giant aubergine – literally opening it up and climbing inside. We had to prise her out with a crowbar."

In order not to upset her too much, Witchy transferred the student to Beginners Voodoo. She took it well, although it's been noticed that her first doll looks incredibly like her former tutor.

Ghosts of Picnics Past

There are some prehistoric stones near Shawley Nott, which are said to be haunted by the ghosts from a picnic in 1930. Usually it's just the food that disappears, but on that occasion four villagers disappeared too. Some say the picnic accessories were possessed, and eerie voices are often heard muttering 'Give me the pickled onions', 'Of course I'd love a bun' and 'Help! I'm being attacked by a cake stand.' The ghosts are known to be extremely angry and aggressive, but as PC Willis says "So would I be if I'd spent 80 years eating the same sandwiches."

One villager claims that she encountered the ghosts whilst taking a stroll near the stones last year. She was found locked in a large picnic basket. When released, she had a sausage roll in each ear, and was smeared all over with jam and marmalade. "I tried to fight them, she advised, "but I found myself being hampered."

Controversy has never been far from the ancient site, which has a central construction consisting of a large slab on four legs. Professor Nigel Beeswax thinks it was used to sacrifice naked virgins, but most of us think it was a picnic table. We found the Professor's call to test his theory a bit disconcerting, not least the way he kept stuttering and trembling when he said the word 'naked'. The picnic aspect connects with our present-day annual summer outing, with rituals such as 'The Slicing of the Plums', 'The Swatting of the Wasps', 'The Popping-open of the Tupperware' and, of course, the dance to worship Thermos, the god of hot liquids.

10. October

Contacting aliens by Radio Transmission

In the following interview, Shawley Nott resident Simpson Bathrobe explains his lifelong quest to contact alien species to Shawley Nott journalist Newton 'Inky' Penn:

Penn: Do you broadcast on a particular frequency?

Bathrobe: Yes, about twice a week.

Penn: I meant with the radio.

Bathrobe: Of course with the radio! Otherwise I wouldn't be able to transmit anything, would I? And if I didn't transmit, how would the aliens hear me? The whole thing becomes absurd. I might as well stand on the top of the hill and wave flags at the stars. It would be a complete waste of time. And I should know because I did that for three years with no results whatsoever.

Penn: But what about hertz?

Bathrobe: Yes, sometimes it hurts. I broadcast at night, and the number of times I've got my foot caught down a rabbit burrow doesn't bear thinking about. That hurts. And I was once attacked by a badger. That hurt even more.

Penn: I meant broadcasting hertz?

Bathrobe: No, I prefer not to broadcast my suffering. I just get on with attempting alien contact.

Penn: No! Hertz! The transmission! Sound waves!

Bathrobe: Oh I see. I chose a high pitch, beyond the capacity of the human ear.

Penn: So how do you know it's working properly?

Bathrobe: Because after a few minutes I'm surrounded by dogs from the village.

Penn: Is it fair to say that contact has been elusive?

Bathrobe: From the perspective of aliens, yes. But I have found a new canine companions and we now get on so well that I've named them. There's Scruffy Bernie, Dribbler, One Ear....

Penn: Is there a time issue? The aliens could reply tomorrow to a transmission you sent two years ago.

Bathrobe: If they did, I'd consider it rude. Bad manners, in fact. Besides, I can't go tomorrow – I've got a darts match.

Penn: But what about the complexities of time and space?

Bathrobe: I wouldn't call them complexities. My time is given freely, and there's plenty of space on the hill, even with the dogs.

Penn: So do you think an alien could be sitting on a hill on a far-away planet transmitting to us?

Bathrobe: I think it's unlikely. You have to consider that you need fingers to work the knobs properly. With suckers and tentacles I'd say it was virtually impossible.

Simpson Bathrobe's book, 'Sending Signals And Barking', is as yet unavailable.

Spontaneous Non-Combustion

Strangely, nobody in Shawley Nott has ever burst into flames. We do discount old Sam Horsenkart, who was warming himself by an open hearth in the pub when he apparently combusted, but this was later deemed to have been his boot spurs striking a spark on the fire grate compounded by the danger of wearing very baggy, flammable, corduroy trousers. Also discounted is Dora Noggs, whose iron ankle clasps struck together while she was running round her bedroom and unfortunately setting light to her stockings.

A brief fire on the village allotments was due to one unscrupulous resident developing a self-igniting lettuce, whilst the explosion that blew glass all over the crops has been pinned on an allotment owner who had eaten a large turkey and sprout pie, then lit a cigarette whilst tending his tomatoes. The fire brigade blamed greenhouse gases.

Possessed by Demons

Demons have possessed many individuals in Shawley Nott, so much so that spirits may be coming up from the underworld through the bathroom pipes. The following cases give an overview of some of the visitations:

Eileen Bunkbed – was possessed by a native American Indian chief called Rampant Buffalo. She insisted on living in a tepee and often arrived at Council meetings wearing a headdress. "It certainly brightened up affairs," commented the Chairman, "although an objection to her warpaint almost put her in tears. We had no idea the spirit possession had terminated. We had to politely suggest that she applied her make up with a little less enthusiasm in future."

Norman Paddelsteamer – for three weeks last summer Norman was possessed by a Roman centurion, curiously named Givvus Atenna. Proved relatively harmless, but kept complaining that many village streets weren't straight enough.

George Leggitt – was strangely possessed by the spirit of Sprinter, a greyhound. His wife found that the quickest way to get him off to work was to stand him in the garage then suddenly raise the garage door. "Sometimes I didn't see him for dust," she explained.

Brenda Prendergast – claimed she was possessed by Satan himself, and that she was voicing his demands. However, the possession was exposed when Satan's main objective became trying to negotiate a 25% discount in the village shop. Despite being threatened with eternal damnation, the shopkeeper insisted Brenda put every item in her basket back where it came from.

On no! Sausage Trolls!

Shawley Nott boasts an unusual family of three Sausage Trolls, who live along the riverbank. All appear to have wild hair and a thin pastry skin over a body of meat.

Hamish is the first. His hair has a tartan appearance, he shares nothing, and is particularly wild. In the village he's known as the Selfish Savage Scottish Sausage Troll, although his name is rarely mentioned because it's too difficult to say.

Slimey is the second. He never washes, and declares 'Soap is the work of the devil' several times daily. But as everyone knows, nothing repeats quite as much as a greasy Sausage Troll. The third, Barria, patrols the river bridge and only lets people cross if they pay him with sausages. He's known as the Sausage Toll Sausage Troll. A group of residents now walk around Shawley Nott every night to prevent the trolls from entering the village. They are known as the Troll Patrol.

"They're very small and quick, and there's nothing they like better than to hide in your underpants," claims Burton McVitie, author of Shawley Nott's best-selling troll book,

'Trolls Where You Least Expect To Find Them'. "They also love bathroom cabinets and chaos. In fact, Barria got into Eileen Bunkbed's bathroom cabinet and squirted a can of shaving foam all over her face. She staggered to the street, but before she could explain what had happened she was put in isolation for six weeks by the local vet on suspicion of rabies."

Ouija Board Tales. Is there anyone out there?

The following is a transcript is Mabel Thyroid speaking about Shawley Nott's Ouija Board group and some of the its recent communication difficulties:

"We use an upturned glass to guide us to the letters. We all place our fingers on the base and the 'spirits' move it back and forth. But last week when we asked "Are you there?" the answer spelled "Sprouts". "Are you a spirit?" brought the result "Aubergine", and for "Do you want to speak to anyone?" the reply was "Spinach". We think the nearby overhead power cables are causing havoc with spirit communication. Either that or we managed to contact a deceased vegetable fetishist.

"Oddly, similar questions the previous night elicited the answers 'yppt', 'gryxt' and 'magortzy'. It remains open as to whether we contacted an alien, a drunk, or as Miss Sminge suggested, a Hungarian. There have been accusations of glass-shoving and the village Indian restaurant owner was banned after the question "What shall we do to smooth our path to the spirit world?" brought forth the answer "Try a tandoori".

"Our most tiring night was when Norman over-varnished the wooden ouija board and the glass moved like a hover-mower. We asked a spirit if there was anything we could do for it and by the time the glass stopped moving we'd got a recipe for chocolate muffins.

"A previous board was hand crafted by Ted, the village carpenter, but in his enthusiasm for the carving he neglected to include the letter 'n'. Nevertheless, we still managed to contact such illustrious individuals as Presidents Abraham Licol and Richard Ixo, actor Errol Fly, Big Crosby, French emperor Apoleo, and Wisto Churchill.

"Our current board is also a little unusual as it's been crafted with a 'yes' option, a 'no', and a 'uh-huh-huh'. The last was included at my insistence, so that Elvis has the easiest path possible if he wishes to communicate with us."

11. November

Supernatural Possession – Donkey Dance

Are Herb Cloggs' donkeys possessed? And if not, how are they learning to dance? Herb Cloggs and his Synchronized Donkey Dancing Troupe are famous throughout Shawley Nott and performed at our recent fiesta (see July).

"I had to experiment, but it was Mambo rhythms that made their ears prick up. They moved in unison across the field, stepping in sequence – it was a miracle. And for the climax they formed a pyramid," Herb explains. "Some people say the donkeys look absurd in sequined leotards, but show business is show business, and the whole spectacular is called Th'Ass Entertainment."

Herb has now taught them several routines. One donkey called Norris can tap dance and has the good fortune that his top hat can double as a small vertical food trough. "People don't realise the potential of donkeys. It's not just dancing – I'm currently training an archery team, a speed skater, and two of them to ride a tandem," adds Herb.

The donkeys have won a number of certificates, but have unfortunately eaten them all. However, some villagers still think the animals are possessed. "There's something wrong…" says Mrs Blenkinsop, "..when a row of donkeys stands up, links front legs, and does the can-can down the High Street. A shiver went down my spine. It has to be witchcraft, which would also explain the unicycling sheep in 2007. Mind you, the sequins looked nice."

The donkeys are so well known that if they go in the village shop they have to wear dark glasses so as not to be recognized. "They give themselves away though," explains the owner, "because they're the only ones in the queue with a basket full of carrots."

The Hound from Hell and Beaver Fever

The moors around Lord Harbinger's estate are said to be the haunt of a savage hound, although witnesses have described him as 'shaggy and ginger'. Rumours say that it may have been a lost puppy brought up by wolves, now heavily troubled by adoption issues. It is said to live in a large cave, the door to which is controlled within Lord Harbinger's mansion. The door mechanism is supposedly linked to his Lordship's drinks cabinet and opens every time he pours himself a whisky. If that's true, then the poor hound could be released up to eighteen times a night.

Over the years, several individuals have been found on the moors with their throats ripped out, although it's known that the moor sheep can also turn nasty.

Norris Ticklestone is the only surviving villager to have witnessed the beast. "I heard paws pounding against the rocks, I turned round, and there he was – a great bundle of shaggy ginger fur steaming towards me. I threw my walking stick, which flew over his head, and then I sprinted home. At first, the beast seemed to run in the opposite direction, but later it almost caught me up, and even tried the front door of my house during the night. I say it howled wildly, but my wife says it whimpered longingly. There was some small consolation the next morning because I found my stick on the doorstep."

It's not just the moors that hide a savage beast. In the 13th century, the river was home to a savage beaver, that mercilessly killed visitors and used their bones for a human dam. Despite the horrific nature of the project, the beaver's artistic talent was widely admired as a complicated construction technique meant the water flowed spectacularly through the jaws of several skulls. The most inept attempt to slay the animal was by a Norwegian visitor, Roger Rogerrogerrogersson, whose weapon of choice was a large wooden club. The beaver used it as a starter before making Roger the main course.

Off record, even a simple bite from the beaver would cause beaver fever, after which victims would return to the village and devour their furniture.

Burnt, baked and singed

Bonfire Night is always a grand occasion in Shawley Nott, although we are aware that ours differs from the usual celebration. We don't burn an effigy of Guy Fawkes, but rather Sydney Gubbins, the village baker in the mid 19th century. It seems a harsh action for what was a matter of poor quality loaves, but the village squire at the time was known for his black humour and nothing would have amused him more than the punishment for bad bread being a damn good toasting. Some say the ghost of Mr Gubbins still haunts the village, and although there have been no sightings, there is an occasional smell of burnt yeast wafting down the High Street.

The village Master of Ceremonies is 'Hugh The Fuse', who makes his own fireworks and has very little body hair. His enthusiasm for his art is infamous - last year he hammered the unfortunately named Catherine Wheel to the pub fence, then lit and spun her. She is, however, 78 years old and has yet to see the funny side of it. Hugh's finest year was 1978, with only seven injured parties. Perhaps the most traumatic event occurred in 1986 when a village school teacher gave a confusing history lesson, saying that every year we should burn one old guy. The children stormed outside in a flash, but the quick action of PC Willis meant pensioner Albert Oblong escaped their pyre with only minor singeing.

Psychic Selection

We feel Shawley Nott's selection of psychic creatures is particularly impressive. In addition to Figgy, the Psychic hamster (see January), the village is proud to be home to:

Syd and Betty, the Psychic Prawns – kept by Cissie Spankington, the prawns waltz around their tank as a prediction of stormy weather. "You'd think the fact that they can waltz would be enough," says Cissie, "but to have psychic weather knowledge is incredible. Mind you, they can also play darts. Not bad for prawns."

Bert the Psychic Moth – "He was incredibly psychic about the danger of electricity," claims his owner, Spindel von Bindel. "Whenever I switched on a light, there he was, fluttering round, warning me that it was hot and dangerous. Unfortunately last week he flew too close, there was a 'pzzzzzt', and he dropped vertically onto the carpet."

Malcolm the Psychic Mole – "His molehills definitely spell out words on my lawn," states Colonel Fizzy Minster, "although we're not sure what he's trying to predict. Words to date include 'it', 'ot', 'dit', 'dot' and 'strawberry mousse'."

Daphne the Psychic Duck – "I scatter bread in the garden," explains Mrs Nitty Tarmack, "making sure half of the pieces are by a sign saying 'hot', and half by a sign saying 'cold'. Whichever bread Daphne eats the most is how my husband takes his lunchtime soup." Despite looking as though this is decision-making rather than being psychic, Nitty disagrees. "I actually ask my husband which he would prefer before Daphne the Duck starts, and fifty percent of the time she gets it right."

Ron the Psychic Badger – "Every night he's psychic about when it gets dark," confesses our village badger expert, "and out he comes."

Debbie the Psychic Snail – "We're still not sure, but she's heading in the right direction," says Mabel Thyroid. Mabel placed two boxes in her garden to predict the weather on Christmas Day. One contains the word 'snow', the other 'no snow'. "I can say she's heading in the right direction because the prediction was intended for Christmas 1998. Perhaps placing the boxes 500m away was asking a bit much, even for a potentially psychic snail."

Plagues Upon Ye – Zombies, Torturers or what?

Shawley Nott has had its fair share of odd plagues over the years. Moist Toe, of course, was originally believed to be a sign of witchcraft, although now it's generally accepted as a consequence of non-leather footwear. Unfortunately, the connection wasn't made quickly enough to save Love Sponge, a hippy who was dunked in the village pond in the late 1960s.

There was also Andrea Listless, whose rich parents had a personal physician attend her daily for ten years to resolve her chest and breathing problems. It turned out she was allergic to stethoscopes. And in mid-December 1910 one villager suffered from a horrific case of facial boils. He was never cured, but went on a ten-day reign of terror every Christmas after acquiring a large piece of mistletoe. Only a few years ago we suspected a large group of residents were suffering from Sheep Syndrome, whereby if one of them decided to do something all of the others followed. However, Dr Grogg later diagnosed this as boredom, and wrote his one and only prescription for tickets to the village bingo.

There have been countless phantoms implicated in phantom pregnancies, as well as Darren the carpenter. Darren isn't a phantom, but then none of the pregnancies associated with him were either.

Poor Brian Treewitch went down with KARSI (Keen to Act and Recreate the Spanish Inquisition), but his wife refused to have him treated as she found his stories about torture chambers more exciting than his usual ones about golf. She only changed her mind after a small disagreement about cleaning the kitchen led to her being hung upside down from their lounge wall in ankle chains.

The 1970s brought the biggest crisis, with so many men dressing identically that it was believed many had become mindless zombies. There was a suspicion that reclusive German veteran Helmut Bankrobbe was trying to start a master race, until it became apparent that beige flares, long hair and multi-coloured tank tops were a fashion trend.

Finally, Miriam Molehill recently thought her husband, Melville, had the medieval sweating sickness, until Dr Grogg proved the symptoms only became apparent when Melville had to open his wallet.

Helicopter Training School for Rabbits

Captain Biggles Chingford, owner of Shawley Nott's Helicopter Training School for Rabbits, offered the following interview to local journalist Newton 'Inky' Penn:

Penn: Captain Chingford, why rabbits?

Chingford: Well, what's the first thing you think about when I say the word 'rabbit'?

Penn: Carrots?

Chingford: No.

Penn: Er.. big ears?

Chingford: No. One more.

Penn: Bugs Bunny?

Chingford: Good Lord no! You're not even trying. It's tunnelling!

Penn: Tunnelling?

Chingford: Yes. You see, when the enemy knows we're training rabbits, they're immediately going to think about an underground operation. But I'm training them to be helicopter pilots. Surprise, I think you'll find, will be ours.

Penn: And how many flights have the rabbits made?

Chingford: To date, thirty two.

Penn: And how many failures?

Chingford: Let me think…one, two, three……..thirty one.

Penn: So you've had one success?

Chingford: Well, I'd use the word 'success' with caution. Ultimately, we won't know until we find the helicopter and rabbit in question.

Penn: Do you use normal helicopters?

Chingford: Don't be absurd. The little chaps could never reach the controls. They just don't have the stretchability. I specially design small helicopters. With an ejector seat.

Penn: An ejector seat?

Chingford: Indeed. It's only fair to the rabbit.

Penn: But…have the seats been tested?

Chingford: On one occasion, yes. But we had some teething problems.

Penn: And how did you find the rabbit?

Chingford: Beautifully sliced. So I'm now working on ejector seats that eject horizontally. We've done a few tests, but the biggest problems have been hillsides and large trees. Of course, flights are limited, because by the time I've dressed all the rabbits in flying jackets and goggles it's often too dark to take off. And they're still tending to nibble the pages of my training manuals. Still, if at first you don't succeed....

Captain Chingford's pamphlet, 'Bob-tailed Bandits', is in preparation.

12. December

Four Horsemen of the Alot-of-dips

As a consequence of a slightly dim wizard in the village, instead of being cursed with the four horsemen of the Apocalypse, Shawley Nott gets the four horsemen of the Alot-of-dips. Rather like the Headless Horse Horseman (see April), they choose to rampage down the high street in their own fashion, although their speed is somewhat hindered by their large tubs of thick dips. On the last occasion, Daphne Polltwanger was caught by surprise and completely blue cheesed. Perhaps the worst incident was when the Horsemen all dressed as Mexicans, and guacamoled every the duck on the village pond.

"On any dark night, to hear the thunder of hooves against the road fills you with terror," says Puffer Watkins. "Old Nobby Streatham barely had time to turn round before he was up to his neck in taramasalata. Mind you, we're not ones to waste food, so he appreciated it when each passerby took a celery stick or a piece of pitta bread and used him as a human dip. He was completely clean in about six weeks."

Our most creative villager made a shield entirely of crackers and after protecting herself from a large dollop of the horsemen's hummus, she ran a surprise buffet at one of her Hen-Taunting nights. Syd Thrupple tried to follow the horsemen on his moped, but skidded on a dollop of an unidentified lumpy brown dip - although given the involvement of four horses, it's hoped that's what it was.

The dim wizard met with an unfortunate end. He claimed he could conduct lightning, but in rushing out to meet a storm he mistakenly picked up his solid iron wand and after waving it hopelessly in the air for ten minutes he suddenly conducted 40,000 volts.

Dangers of Demon Possession (Fridge Dept)

Mabel Thyroid had a bit of a struggle on her hands last week when she opened her fridge door only to be attacked by the contents, which seemed to have been possessed by fridge demons. It's not the first time that products have become possessed, and fridge magnets may be attracting them. As Mabel ran from her kitchen with a string of sausages tightening around her neck and several rashers of bacon slapping at her backside, her husband rose to the demon challenge and fended off a dozen eggs with a cricket bat. Unfortunately, he was then felled by a chicken wing, which glided in unseen from the direction of the chandelier. "When he went down, I thought we'd had our chips," stated Mabel, "but they were next out of the icebox and came at me like bullets."

The muesli yogurt then went for the cat just as the cat went for the sardines, but the sardines were to strong for him and pinned him to the cupboard door. The whole affair shook Mabel up completely, but not half as much as the semi-skimmed milk, not refrigerated at the time, which was so shook up it turned to butter.

"Fridge demons are evil," advised Mabel's husband upon regaining consciousness, "The worst aspect was the magnetic alphabet letters on the fridge door. We normally spell things we've run out of, like milk or bread, but after the demons had vanished the message read 'We'll be back'."

Psychic Pets Competition

After the flurry of psychic creatures recently (see November), the village's Psychic Pets Competition rolled around again last weekend. It was, unpredictably, chaos. Reg Mildew's psychic melon was disqualified on the grounds that it wasn't a pet at all, despite Reg's protests that he took it for walks and called it Fluffy. A psychic Persian cat that could read the mind of its 103-year-old owner was also ruled out through lack of evidence, although they certainly dozed off at the same time on a number of occasions.

A psychic chameleon was impressive. It correctly changed its colour to correspond with that of concealed circular cards, which were either red, amber or green, but unfortunately someone then left it facing the village traffic lights and it died of exhaustion. A psychic goat that was claimed to bleat in the event of an attack by flying cows remained untested, as was a guinea pig that apparently tap-danced as a prediction of a drop in the pound/dollar exchange rate.

Noreen Snibbles psychic hawk went skywards to read the future from cloud shapes, but unfortunately got distracted by Cheesy, the psychic field mouse. If Cheesy did have a premonition about his own death then he didn't move anywhere near quickly enough.

Midgeley Snetterton's psychic chicken, Vernon, failed miserably to foresee the danger in its master's journey home. Midgeley stepped on a spring-loaded drain cover and was hurled through the air into a threshing machine.

The winner was deemed to be Lana, the psychic lamb. She didn't turn up for the competition, but in view of the fact that Syd Snarling unexpectedly brought his three psychic wolves, that was proof enough for the judges.

Oh Village Sage…

Every ten years Shawley Nott's Village Sage is wheeled out under our historic oak tree (see June) to answer questions that are worrying residents. The Sage is believed to be more than 250 years old, has one eye, and his strangely styled white hair (with one long upward tuft) and beard (with two long downward tufts) now almost cover his face. As Frothy Dinsdale commented, "it's a bit like talking to the rear end of a Persian cat." The following conversation details his latest appearance, with questions from villagers Bob, Bernard and Cheryl:

Cheryl: Oh sage, how do I mend a broken heart?

Sage: Who broke it?

Cheryl: My boyfriend.

Sage: Well then he should mend it.

Cheryl: But we're not speaking….

Sage: Don't argue. I'm a Sage. I know what I'm talking about.

Cheryl: But…

Sage: Next question!

Bob: What colour should I paint my shed?

Sage: Brown.

Bob: Brown?

Sage: No, wait a minute…maroon.

Bob: Maroon? That's a bit odd for a shed. Why maroon?

Sage: Because I'm a wise old sage and I said so.

Bob: But my wife doesn't like maroon.

Sage: Well then you should've asked what colour your wife wants you to paint the shed, shouldn't you?

Bernard: What about some philosophy questions? What's the secret of eternal life?

Sage: Blue.

Bernard: Blue is the secret of eternal life?

Sage: What? No! Blue is the colour his wife wants him to paint his shed. I got confused. It's not easy, all this….sageing. Can't a 250-year-old sage get confused if he wants?

Bob: I thought we were meant to ask you questions?

Sage: You are.

Bob: But you just asked us if you could get confused.

Sage: It was rhetorical! Next!

Cheryl: Should I telephone my boyfriend?

Bob: Doesn't my wife want the shed painted olive green?

Bernard: What about eternal life?

Sage: One at a time! Is that too much to ask?

Bob: Er… was that rhetorical or not?

Sage: All of my questions are rhetorical! I'm a Sage. Is that clear?

(There is silence.)

Sage: I said is that clear?

Bob: So that question wasn't rhetorical?

Sage: No.

Bob: Yes.

Sage: How dare you! The answer is no!

Bob: I know, but I was answering 'yes' to 'Is that clear?' There's no need to get shirty.

Sage: I can't believe I get wheeled out every ten years for this.

Bob: I'm sure my wife wants the shed olive green.

Cheryl: I think I'll phone my boyfriend tonight.

Bernard: I'm not sure I want the secret of eternal life. I get bored at weekends now. Actually, this is a bit like questioning the rear end of a Persian cat.

Sage: That's enough. Can someone take me home please?

Zombie Employment Agency

"I just got fed up with them hanging around the village, arms dangling lifelessly at their sides, and occasionally grunting," explains village entrepreneur Mavis Haggle. "So I set up the Zombie Employment Agency to offer them jobs. Even dead-end ones, which they're rather suited to, actually."

Mavis has a good eye for business, whereas some of the zombies just have a good eye. "I've tried to teach them to talk rather than to grunt or wail," Mavis continues, "but invariably when they speak their teeth tend to fall out. Also, decomposition can be a problem. I shook hands with one of them, he left the office and when I went to use my keyboard I realised that I still had his hand in mine. That was quite a shock I can tell you. When I let go, it scuttled across the desk and went for Possum, the office cat. However, we've managed to place three zombies as scarecrows, and one as a shop mannequin. Surprisingly, the majority have been employed as Customer Service representatives. Apparently, they're good at handling complaints, because after several grunts and no human reaction at all, those complaining just give up. The village bank employs four."

In order to find more zombies, the council authorised members of the Shawley Nott Football Club to stand with shovels in the graveyard in order to help any zombie looking to rise through the turf. But when a few zombies broke through, the players panicked and used their shovels to smack the zombies over the head. "I don't want to expand on the zombies reactions," explains Mavis, "but afterwards most of the first eleven could dig a trench to their rear by simply bending and straightening their knees. You can't say zombies don't have a sense of humour."

Shawley Nott Scream Club

"It's no good being scared if you don't scream properly," says the President of Shawley Nott's Scream Club. "Following a sighting of the Headless Horse Horseman (see April), one villager screamed like a constipated otter. And after catching sight of the Brotherhood of the Headless Chicken (see May), another hit such a high-pitched note that three bats dropped dead from the church eaves. It's just not on. And what's more, I don't expect to arrive at a scene with a silver bullet in my revolver to find a villager disturbed by Nifty Briscoe standing naked in the bushes. Nifty shouldn't merit a werewolf-type scream, no matter what he's exposing. Anyway, I started the Scream Club so that we could practice screams that reflect the nature of the distress."

Apparently, several villagers go to the monthly practice, although Enid Schwarzenhoppen has been banned for yodelling, which was defined as a cause of screaming rather than a scream itself.

The club secretary, Major Voyce-Box, has instituted scream grading, from one to five, based on pitch, duration and variation of tone. Cyril Tonnage has failed miserably to achieve any form of consistency, although his efforts have won him the role of Tarzan in the village drama society production of Tarzan versus Godzilla. Doreen Growler will be reprising her role as Godzilla, having seen off Roger Trubshaw's King Kong over three nights last year.

The Major explains: "When I hear a scream, I want to know why. A grade five is a vampire or werewolf threat, whereas grade two could be a witch. I attended an incident last month when Sybil Primanpropper screamed to level three because she'd found her husband wearing her clothes again. We forgave her, and frankly having witnessed his appearance, I'm surprised she didn't go higher."

13. Shawley Nott's Olympic Bid

An interview with the Mayor

Having witnessed the spectacular efforts of Beijing and London, Shawley Nott's Mayor felt the village should prepare a bid to host the Olympic Games. In this rare interview, he puts forward his suggestions about how the village could rise to the occasion, under the proposed slogan, 'Eliminating Hurdles and Crossing the Line':

Interviewer: Is Shawley Nott really able to compete with cities such as Beijing and London?

Mayor: Well, let's not forget those cities needed to construct an Olympic village. Of course, Shawley Nott is already a village, so we won't need to construct anything.

Interviewer: But what about facilities?

Mayor: We all had a chat in the pub last night, and we think the only problem could be the marathon, which I believe is about twenty-six miles. Since it's one mile round the village, contestants could run around twenty-six times, but we were slightly concerned about them getting dizzy. We think the village pond is big enough for swimming and Miss Webfoot has promised to try to isolate the ducks. The school playing fields could host athletics, with gymnastics in the village hall. We'd also like to introduce what we call 'MBEs' - Mutually Beneficial Events - such as Olympic Church Renovation, Olympic Cream Tea Consumption and an Olympic Jumble Sale.

Interviewer: And I understand you'd like to change some sports to make the whole thing more jolly?

Mayor: Yes. For us, it's all got a bit too competitive. So, for the relay, we'd establish a rule whereby you can only pass the baton to an athlete in an opposing team. Wouldn't that be a great way for athletes from different nations to meet each other? We'd also like to see a bit more fun, so we would add a Sack Race, and an Egg and Spoon Race. It also seems to me that some events are very long for the competitors - not just the marathon, but the five and ten thousand metres - so we'd introduce little cafés on route in each of those.

Interviewer: But won't the competitors be concentrating on winning?

Mayor: Not at our Olympics because we've decided that the medals should be given out before a race starts so that competitors can really concentrate on the enjoyment of taking part.

Interviewer: But who wins?

Mayor: Under those circumstances, we all do!

Interviewer: And I trust you've something special planned for the opening ceremony?

Mayor: Oh yes. Members of the Shawley Nott HandBell Ringing Society are going to play the national anthem of every country in the world, consecutively.

Interviewer: Won't that take quite along time?

Mayor: Well, we're going to try to achieve it in less than three days. There have already been practices, but unfortunately in the first Mrs Lobe lost track after Belgium, and in the second Mr Mordin collapsed in the middle of Latvia. We've come to the conclusion a small break may be needed in Jamaica.

Interviewer: And accommodation?

Mayor: All visitors will be given a sleeping bag and allocated to a Shawley Nott resident. It worked perfectly well for the children evacuated here during World War Two. Obviously, nowadays there would be no obligation to work in the fields, but in the event that we needed some potatoes dug or strawberries picked, we trust offers would be forthcoming.

Interviewer: What about the press?

Mayor: Do you mean the nasty wooden thing with screws in the village Torture Museum?

Interviewer: No – I mean tv, reporters and the internet?

Mayor: Don't worry – the village pub has wifi.

Interviewer: And the closing ceremony?

Mayor: Harold, our highly experienced Balloon Modeller, is planning something special.

Interviewer: It may be unlikely, but what happens if you win the bid?

Mayor: Well, we would immediately put our Master Olympic Operation, or MOO for short, into action. It's a five-point document that can be seen on the wall of my office.

Interviewer: Have you calculated a budget?

Mayor: Indeed. At the moment it stands at £152.75.

Interviewer: That seems a little on the low side.

Mayor: I would agree, but you have to remember that there are still funds to come in from the sponsored Witch Trials and the Possessed Cheese competition.

Interviewer: Don't you mean Processed Cheese?

Mayor: No, Possessed Cheese. There is a famous event in the UK whereby villagers chase a large, circular cheese down a hill. Following a slight disagreement here with the Great Village Cheese Wizard in 1952, a lot of our cheese is still possessed, so it can run up a hill, which makes the pursuit more tiring. As you can imagine, a strong cheese can take your breath away, but the men of the village are usually triumphant.

Interviewer: So the village is prepared. What would be the best way of describing a Shawley Nott Olympic Triumph This Year?

Mayor: SNOTTY.

Interviewer: Thank you.

Mayor: My pleasure. I'll have to dash because I've just heard there's been a bit of a nasty accident during a javelin test.